sin

Health

Christopher Herbert

DARTON·LONGMAN + TODD

First published in 2012 by
Darton, Longman and Todd Ltd
1 Spencer Court
140 – 142 Wandsworth High Street
London SW18 4JJ

The right of Christopher Herbert to be identified as the author of this
work has been asserted in accordance with the Copyright, Designs and
Patents Act 1998.

ISBN: 978-0-232-52886-2

A catalogue record for this book is available from the British Library.

Phototypeset by Judy Linard
Printed and bound by GZ Digital Media

Contents

Introduction:
The nature of health

YOU MAY HAVE come across Mrs Pendlebury. She is a harridan, a nagging, elderly woman with a particularly feeble, stubborn and scheming husband called Stanley. Her life is confined almost entirely to her house and garden in a suburb of North London. In her small kingdom she is undoubtedly the Boss. Outside it, however, she is afraid even to cross the road.

Stanley Pendlebury, a retired office worker, seems to spend a considerable amount of self-pitying time at the doctor's where he rehearses a litany of minor complaints. Rose Pendlebury, by contrast, is, for much of the time, the acme of apparent health. She scrubs and polishes and gardens with furious zeal. Her life, however, is emotionally and intellectually narrow, but then something happens which has a significant effect upon her and she begins to blossom. For a while she tries to see herself and other people in a new light.

Gradually, however, as bad luck intervenes, some of her old habits of mind reassert themselves and she spirals downwards into a dark and terrible breakdown.

The novel in which Rose and Stanley Pendlebury are to be found is written by Margaret Forster, and is a study in misconceptions, the virtues and vices of the human heart and of a relationship which is doggedly and, at the end, tragically human.

One of the underlying themes of the novel concerns the nature of the health and well-being of individuals, and what happens when carefully constructed 'worlds' and relationships sway and crumble (or not) under duress.

Health, in this novel, is not simply about physical well-being (though, in fact, Stanley suffers an unpleasant and ignominious episode of physical trauma); it is also about healthy and unhealthy relationships, the impact of fate and chance, and the ways in which the characters cope with what life flings at them.

It might have been expected that a book such as this one, dedicated to exploring health and well-being, would have begun with a careful definition of what we mean by 'health' or 'well-being', but I chose to begin with the characters from a novel because they show that health is inevitably bound up not only with the proper functioning of our bodies, but also with our relationships, the society and culture in which we live, and with our own self-understanding. Let me put it another way. It might be perfectly reasonable to describe someone as 'healthy' whose body does not function very well but who brings much joy and fulfilment to people whom they meet. Conversely, it is just as reasonable to describe someone as 'unhealthy' who works out at the gym regularly and has a well-balanced diet, but whose relationships are in a mess and who bullies everyone around.

If health is not limited just to our bodies, it is worth going on to ask about some of the deeper elements of our human-ness. Put it this way: can we, or should we, consider what we might call our *spiritual* health? The question is an entirely open one. I hesitate to ask it, because it might lead to an unhealthy introspection or to scrupulosity, and yet, we know that the secret and deep recesses of our hearts are a profound part of who we are and help to shape and determine our lives. Take time for a moment to consider your soul, your innermost being. As you do so, you may find yourself coming up against an insistent question: 'Is my soul simply (simply?) a product of my human experience, or is there a relationship between my soul and God?'

I leave the question with you. It is one to mull over, to ponder. If you come to the conclusion that there is indeed a relationship between your innermost being and God, ask him to help you to be in a good and fruitful relationship with him and with other people, so that the deepest wellsprings of your life might flourish.

You might want to consider finding a wise person who will be your 'soul friend', that is, someone who is especially concerned with the deepest workings of our human personalities, a spiritual director. If you do not know someone already, ask your priest, vicar or minister if they can suggest someone to whom you might turn to explore these questions.

1

The nature of suffering

FROM TIME TO TIME an event happens in our world which shakes us to the core. I think, for example, of the Boxing Day tsunami in 2004, and the Japanese earthquake and tsunami in 2010. It is the sheer destructive power of these things which is overwhelming, and even seasoned journalists struggle to describe what they see – whole communities obliterated, individuals numb with terror and shock, squatting on their haunches among the wreckage.

How can suffering on such a scale and operating with such indifference be consistent with a God whom Christians describe as Love? The question is sharp and insistent and should not be avoided.

There are a number of ways of trying to answer. The first and simplest is to deny the existence of God. If there is no God, then when suffering happens, it is just the way things are: earthquakes happen, fires burn, diseases are rampant. And while we as humans might want to respond courageously and self-sacrificially to lessen their effects, there's no need to ask theological questions. Such questions, in this view, are literally, non-sense. Put crudely, no God, no problem.

A second answer is to suggest that there is a God,

the Creator, but he is indifferent to suffering. We are, as it were, his playthings, and he is an amoral being, a psychopath, who toys with us like a cat toys with a mouse.

The difficulty with this argument is that it ignores what we consider to be virtues, such as goodness and truth, yet these seem to be as much built in to the hardware of our humanity as are their opposites. Would an amoral God have created a world of such moral beauty and complexity?

The third answer is to say that there is a Creator God but he is not all-powerful. He and his creation are under constant attack from a malevolent opponent; suffering is the result of this titanic and universal struggle between Good and Evil, Light and Dark. In such a scenario we have to put up with being pawns in a much bigger struggle, perhaps placating one side or the other. The difficulty with this argument is that while it may be usefully descriptive of what we sometimes feel, it offers no hope, no resolution, and it does not conform to our sense of justice. And it raises the further question of the origin of evil and darkness.

The fourth answer to the question of suffering is closely allied to the previous one. It argues that there is a God who is Creator but he is under attack from an opposing force, the force of evil, otherwise known as the devil. In this scenario there was a time when the earth was a place of perfection but sin entered the fabric of things through human disobedience (the Fall), and the devil thereby achieved an entry into the world and tries constantly and cunningly to assert his control. But at the End of Time, the devil will be defeated by God. Meanwhile, we live in the conflict zone and in that zone, because of the devil's wiles and human disobedience, there is suffering.

This argument has dominated much of western Christian thinking for a very long time. It has given rise to some great works of art, for example, those images of the Last Judgement to be found in medieval churches and cathedrals. And it has led to considerable theological debate about the nature and purpose of Jesus' death. If human beings were disobedient at the Fall, runs the argument, justice demands that they should be punished. However, Jesus took all human sin upon himself on the cross, thereby satisfying the just demands of God.

While this argument has a long history, it does have some weaknesses. For example, who created the devil? And who allows the devil to have so much headroom? If it is God who created the devil and allows him to continue to exercise his power, is it morally right to regard our sin as entirely our own fault?

On the other hand, this traditional argument about the cause of suffering has the strong merit of taking the horrendous nature of suffering and evil seriously; it also offers humankind a sense of moral freedom. We can choose, if we wish, to reject the devil and all his works, and can choose instead to follow the way of God.

The fifth argument related to suffering is to say that God is Creator and suffering is part of his inscrutable purpose for the world. We are, compared with God, mere nothings and cannot begin to understand his divine ways; therefore, when suffering happens we should regard it as part of his unfathomable purpose. We should not question it, but simply accept whatever happens.

This argument takes the ineffable mystery of God seriously, but it fails to take account of our human desire to understand, and to try to combat suffering; more, it can lead to a kind of moral indifference, especially in relation to those who suffer.

The sixth argument says that suffering is the consequence of our failure to live justly and righteously in a previous life. The problem with this approach is that having no awareness of having led a previous life, let alone one in which we apparently lived unjustly, how can we possibly learn from our mistakes? It all seems opaque and arbitrary. Furthermore, it can prevent any sense that we might feel obliged morally to intervene to alleviate suffering.

The seventh argument is to accept that there is a God who is Creator and who, in order to allow virtues such as courage and truthfulness to come into being, has to create a world in which both regularity and chaos are built in to the system. Chaos involves the potential for new things to emerge, but also of things going wrong. If cells are to multiply to create new life forms, for example, then they might not switch themselves off at the correct moment and cancer might be the result. But without risk, newness and development would not be able to occur; without risk, things would remain static, and we, as humans, would have no challenges to face, no opportunities for moral growth. Where there is risk, there is inevitably the possibility of suffering, but without suffering there could be no courage, no love, and no growth in sympathy or moral awareness.

This argument goes on to say that God, having created a world in which suffering is inevitable, enters the suffering himself in order to redeem it. This is what Jesus of Nazareth did on the cross – he revealed the true nature of God, a God who himself is wounded and thereby enters and shares all our suffering.

It seems to me that this argument is the only one which gets close to holding together love, power and the Being of God: that wherever there is suffering, God is in the midst of it, undergoing the agonies with us and ultimately working to bring us wholeness, healing and reconciliation.

It is not possible to do justice to all the nuances and varieties of arguments that exist about the nature of suffering in a chapter as brief as this, but I hope that even this inadequate summary of some of those arguments may help.

I am, however, very conscious that when suffering

strikes, even the most carefully thought-out arguments pale into insignificance. We find ourselves drawn down to a deeper layer of our humanity, where philosophical and theological arguments, such as the ones I have outlined, seem futile, and all we can do is to enter the suffering and pray that God himself will be with us. It is the true experience of many of us that in the deepest darkness there is light, and Christ himself walks with us in our suffering, in love and with the utmost compassion. It is that experience to which I hold.

2

Living with uncertainty

YOU WILL KNOW the scene. It could be any A and E department, anywhere in the country. It is early evening on a Bank holiday Monday.

The place is beginning to fill up. Two men, one of whom is cradling his injured hand, watch a 'soap' on a huge flat-screen television. Next to them, a young woman waits on her own; her face is impassive but her eyes are clouded with anxiety. An old man enters, walks briskly up to the receptionists' desk and asks how long he will have to wait. He is accompanied by his teenage granddaughter whose rubbery tummy flops loosely over the waistband of her faded jeans. She is restless with embarrassment as her grandfather explains loudly that he has cracked a couple of ribs and if he cannot be seen immediately there is no point in staying. A young child, limp in his father's muscular arms, whimpers in pain. In the corner, next to a pile of magazines, an older man is sitting with his wife. He has been brought in by the paramedics and is suspected of having had a mild heart attack. Three young people, two sisters and a brother, are being extravagantly and obscenely noisy, and seem entirely oblivious of the other patients in the room. A teenage youth hops in on one leg, leaning his half-naked and skinny torso against his giggling girlfriend. The receptionists' phones ring constantly. One of them is trying to explain to a caller who has little English how to get to the hospital. The triage nurse, brisk and efficient, calls a patient in to see her. The television soap continues to blather away on the wall.

You will recognise the scene: a place where sudden and unexpected emergencies bring together a cross section of humanity. Each person present began the day not expecting to be waiting there; now, none of them knows what the outcome of their appointment might reveal. Will the child whimpering in pain be kept in overnight? What is actually wrong? Look at his father's arms and shaven head, a tough, strong man, but on his face is written a most tender and aching anxiety. He is, however, not in control.

Will the old man with his cracked ribs become more and more angry with the receptionist, and will his granddaughter who stands with him, but at a little distance, have to cope with his mounting irascibility?

Will the teenage boy, who entered the department hopping on one leg because of a foot injury (which he is treating with a loud and amused bravado), find that the injury is more serious than he currently imagines?

Will the man with a suspected heart attack have to have a major op?

The one thing all these people in this crowded room have in common is uncertainty. The day that for each of them began so ordinarily has been turned upside down and none of them can know, for the moment, how the day will turn out.

In a sense, what A and E departments reveal is a truth about all our lives, that beneath the surface there is uncertainty. It is an inescapable fact of our human condition, which, fortunately, we are not often asked or required to confront, but when we have to, what are the inner resources we have at our disposal?

From very early times churches have used a collective form of prayer called 'litanies' (the word means 'supplications'), in which God is asked to have mercy upon all people. Those litanies often contain a prayer about living with sudden uncertainty. For example, a litany widely used in the English-speaking world since the seventeenth century (and dating from much earlier) contains the petition, 'From lightning and tempest; from plague, pestilence and famine; from battle and murder and sudden death: Good Lord, deliver us.' The petition has a rolling sonority, and through its structure and its rhythms it brings home, even to a casual reader, a sense of awe in the face of potential catastrophe. A recent version says, more prosaically, 'From famine and disaster, from violence, murder and dying unprepared: good Lord, deliver us.'

Those litanies, not as widely used as once they were, have the sobering effect of reminding all those who use them of the uncertainty of life.

But now, in spite of endless news which is, by definition, dominated by the unexpected, we are probably less prepared than our forebears were to cope with the essential fragility of our lives. Perhaps, in our generation, when the abyss of uncertainty is suddenly exposed beneath our feet, we might want to turn to one of the oldest litanies of all, the Kyrie Eleison, and say, 'Lord, have mercy upon us: Christ, have mercy upon us; Lord, have mercy upon us.'

When we do this, we place our own frailty into the hands of our eternally loving, eternally strong God, and rest ourselves there, knowing that God is with us every step of the way.

3

The question of miracles

LOOK. NO MATTER which way we may turn, in a book about health and well-being, we cannot avoid the question of miracles. So, let's try to tackle the question head on.

For me, having read the Bible most of my life, the natural reaction is to go straight to the Bible to try to understand what is meant by miracles there. But I want to postpone that process for the moment and instead try to explore what is meant by miracles today. And the most obvious place to begin is with a definition.

The *Oxford English Dictionary* defines a miracle as 'An extraordinary and welcome event that is not explicable by natural or scientific laws and is therefore attributed to a divine act'. One imagines that such a beautifully constructed definition is the result of rigorous debate in which every word is weighed with judicious and scholarly care. However, as with any definition, it raises almost as many questions as it seems to answer; for example, what exactly is meant by 'natural law' and 'scientific law'?

If you begin from the assumption that everything that happens in the world can be explained by 'natural law', and that even those things that are not yet explicable will be one day, then there is no need to posit an 'outside agent', what the *OED* calls a 'divine act'. Similarly, if you also assume that everything in the world is, in principle, reducible to scientific laws then, again, there is no need to assume the existence of an 'outside agent'. Things are, as it were, what they are and it is our delightful and challenging task as human beings to refine and predict with greater and greater accuracy how the world and the universe work. With sufficient ingenuity and knowledge, extra-ordinary events will be discovered to be ordinary and explicable.

I am not a scientist but what I observe happening in science, and especially in astronomy, is increasing humility in the face of new discoveries and a willingness to stretch imagination and language in order to describe and understand. It is all very exciting, as old ideas are giving way to new.

Notwithstanding the importance of exploring natural law and pushing on the boundaries of scientific endeavour, the question is whether an essentially mechanistic view of the universe is adequate for all circumstances and in all situations. Take, for example, the question of human self-consciousness, what we call 'mind'. When we only use mechanistic terms to describe 'mind' are we certain that we have captured all that there is to say? Put it this way, is the 'me-ness' of 'me' simply and only the inevitable and predictable result of the firing of the synapses in my brain? Or, if you prefer another analogy, are virtues such as courage, love and truthfulness merely the random and fortuitous outcomes of the brain's electro-chemical processes? If they are, what is the point in talking about the morality or otherwise of human behaviour? Perhaps, what we call 'virtues' are hard-wired into our brains, and if they are, then what we call 'vices' might be similarly hardwired. We deserve therefore neither praise for our virtues nor blame for our vices. We are what we are, and our exercise of moral behaviour, as though we have any control over it, is illusory.

Now try this thought experiment. Ask yourself this question: 'Do I actually behave or think as though I am explicable solely in mechanistic terms?' If the answer to the question is 'Yes', then there's no need to proceed any further. You can close this book now, make yourself a cup of coffee and find something else to do with your time. But if the answer is 'No', some implications follow. It implies, doesn't it, that we do not find the mechanistic hypothesis entirely convincing? It implies that life is more complex, more beautiful, more mysterious than any mechanistic theory will allow. In brief, the 'Why?' question is as important as the 'How?' question, and mechanistic views of human identity and behaviour seem not to be able to answer the 'Why?' We may therefore find ourselves moving to a position in which we begin to wonder whether the origin and purpose and destiny of our lives are to be found not in the heavily circumscribed notions of mechanistic theories, but outside ourselves. In brief, we may find ourselves exploring the possibility of God…

Well. This may seem a strange way to approach the question of miracles, but, by definition, the concept of miracle requires, as it were, an 'outside agent'; an activity in which the divine breaks through all the normal rules that govern the way the universe is.

And at this point, you might think that the question boils down to whether or not you believe in God. But, in fact, it gets a little more complicated than that. If, for example, you believe in God, it also means that you need some idea of what characteristics an intervention by God would have to have for it to deserve to be called a divine act. Supposing God to be good, for example, it would require any intervention on his part not to be malicious. More positively, supposing God to be infinite, it would require an intervention to be redolent with new and unforeseen meaning; supposing God to be love, it would require any intervention to be filled with the potential for the participants to become more loving, more God-like.

All of this presupposes a kind of 'distance' between God and the world such that it requires an intervention by God from the 'outside'. But suppose that there is *no* distance between God and the world, but that he is deeply embedded in all that is. After all, it could be argued that God is the Ground of Being, and that he, as it were, contains and enfolds all things. Any talk then of intervention from 'outside' becomes problematic. What this kind of thinking tends to lead towards is the idea that all new insights, all new discoveries, all new understandings are part of the very Being of God, and thus it challenges a strict 'natural' versus 'supernatural' view of the world. It does not preclude a 'divine act', but it does suggest that such acts are part of a continuum.

A further point which is worth considering is whether *any* language about God, whether referring to God as 'outside' or 'inside', is ever adequate. When we talk about God, it seems to me, we always need to watch the language we use to ensure that it is neither too constricting nor misleading.

Be that as it may, when it comes to the question of miracles, it would seem that our approach to it will be determined by two things. First, by our fundamental beliefs about our own self-understanding (are we explicable solely in mechanistic terms, or are there other more fruitful and accurate explanations?); second, by our beliefs about the nature and existence of God. If there is no God, then all talk of miracles is literally non-sense; if, however, there is a God, further questions are raised about whether God can or does intervene in the world's affairs, and if so, why, how and in what circumstances.

Maybe it is time to see how the Bible tackles some of these questions…

4

Miracles and the Bible

WHAT DOES THE Bible, and in particular the New Testament, say about miracles?

If you read the opening chapter of the gospel of Mark, you will find that it consists of no fewer than four stories of healing miracles. There is the public and stormy battle in the synagogue at Capernaum on the Sabbath day when Jesus rebukes what is called an 'unclean spirit' in a man. The man convulses, and with a loud cry the spirit leaves him. There is the domestic, more private setting of a home where Jesus heals Simon Peter's mother-in-law of a fever. There is the situation outside the house in the street, where crowds flock to Jesus to be healed and, says Mark, he 'healed many who suffered from various diseases, and drove out many demons'. And then, finally, there is the moving story of a leper who approaches Jesus and with a heart-felt plea says: 'If only you will, you can make me clean.' Jesus was apparently deeply moved, stretched out his hand, touched the leper and said, 'I will: be clean.' And, Mark continues, 'the leprosy left him immediately, and he was clean'.

It is not a matter of chance that Mark placed these four stories of healings so closely together right at the beginning of his gospel. They are there to create a dramatic, punchy effect: this man Jesus, he seems to be saying, had immense and awesome authority.

The questions for a twenty-first-century reader about Jesus and miracles however, will not go away, no matter how dramatically written the opening of Mark's gospel might be. Take, for example, the miracle in the Capernaum synagogue. In Western Europe the notion that someone might be possessed by 'evil spirits' has not been part of our medical or cultural vocabulary for many centuries. We are distinctly uneasy about it, not least because we have seen how the concept led in earlier centuries, both before and after the Reformation, to appalling injustice and cruelty: think of all those elderly, reclusive women who were burnt alive as witches because they behaved eccentrically and were therefore regarded as being 'possessed'. But tragically, some groups in our country continue to believe in the concept of 'possession', especially in young children, with often appalling consequences. It is not surprising that when such cases come to light, they are met with moral outrage. Furthermore, when we read elsewhere in the gospels of a young boy being 'possessed' by an evil spirit, we recognise the symptoms from which he is suffering (convulsions, foaming at the mouth, grinding his teeth, and falling over), but we describe them as epilepsy, and rightly reject some kind of supernatural cause for the condition. Medical and cultural developments over the past two thousand years mean that we simply do not, cannot and should not inhabit the thought worlds of first-century Palestine.

What then are we to make of Jesus' healing miracles? In those miracles which are related to 'possession', one of the things we need to do is to acknowledge that that form of diagnosis was as natural and normal for first-century Palestine as counselling and psychotherapy are to our generation. Who knows what our successors will make of *our* medical concepts? We should not be too hasty to adopt superior attitudes. What seems to have been going on is that Jesus lived fully within the conceptual and religious framework of his day, just as we do in ours, but responded to it with a profound, disturbing and liberating authority. He did not wish people to be shackled and crippled by the limitations of their own thought-worlds (especially their religious thought-worlds), but wanted to bring them into another place where they might experience the joy and freedom of God. His presence, his voice and his authority ensured that that happened.

In those kinds of healings (for which some might employ the word 'psychosomatic'), the miracle is that there was something about Jesus' presence which was enough to bring people real freedom of mind and soul.

27

We might also want to recognise that although we no longer talk of 'demon possession', we nevertheless use phrases about people being 'in the grip' of unhealthy patterns of behaviour. We talk of people being 'taken over' by their addictions, 'enslaved' by drugs or alcohol or gambling, for example. We refer to people in the passive sense of 'suffering from' morbid thoughts or depression, or whatever their illness might be. In other words, we recognise that many people do not necessarily cause their own condition, but long to be 'liberated' from patterns of behaviour over which they have little control. For such people, a 'miracle' would be the breaking of their shackles.

I am not for one moment suggesting a *simplistic* 'Jesus' answer for such people, but certainly for some the sense of liberation they experience when they read about Jesus, or experience true loving acceptance by others or by God, is for them truly miraculous. God, as it were, becomes the centre and purpose of their being, and that replaces their addiction; while they might never talk of 'cure', preferring, for the sake of honesty, to refer to themselves as 'recovering', the spiritual process of centring more and more on God's love is a true and healing liberation.

We might find therefore that, although we do not inhabit the thought-world of early New Testament times, there are sufficient parallels and echoes in our own experience for us to get closer to an understanding of some of Jesus' miracles, particularly those that seem to have a psychosomatic element.

But what we need to do when reading the gospels is not only to compare them with the cultural concepts of our own day but also to recognise that their authors had their own particular story to tell which they shaped and told in their own unique way. Mark, as I have said, opens his gospel with four healing miracles. By complete contrast, Matthew waits for seven chapters before he mentions a healing miracle (see Matthew 8:1–4). Then, if you read John's gospel, you will find that there are only three or four healing miracles mentioned at all, whereas Luke has at least fifteen. What the gospels do have in common, however, is that none of them mentions any healings in Jesus' last days in Jerusalem. It's an intriguing question as to why this should be. There are also situations, for example in the healing of the blind man Bartimaeus (Mark 10:46–52), where the story is probably placed by Mark where it is in order to prepare the reader to 'see' that in the days that follow people will be spiritually blind and will fail to recognise Jesus for who he truly is. In other words, when we read the healing miracle stories in the gospels we need to be aware of some of the underlying intentions of the authors. Things are frequently more subtle than they might appear to be at first glance. We should read the gospels with intelligence and care and recognise that although the healing miracles may cause us some intellectual disquiet, they are in fact only a small part of the overall story. Our faith does not stand or fall depending on what we think of the miracles. There are much bigger miracles to consider, as the next chapter will suggest.

5

Miracles in our own thinking

BEARING THE CAVEAT in mind in the previous chapter, in which it was stated that the Bible is often more subtle and complex than at first appears, what are we to make of those miracles which seem more to do with the body than the mind or the soul?

Think, for example, of the story of the healing of the leper in that first chapter of Mark's gospel (Mark 1:40–45). It would appear that one minute the man had the disease, and the next, after encountering Jesus, he was entirely cured. We can explore the question by saying that definitions of leprosy then were different from definitions now, and that is true. We might go on to argue that perhaps the man was suffering from some kind of psychosomatic skin disease which responded miraculously to Jesus' liberating presence. That too might be true, and in fact when you look in detail at the healing miracle stories in the gospels the great majority of them fall into the psychosomatic category. But there are some which remain obstinately physical. So how can we explain those?

We have to begin by acknowledging that all we have to go on is the text itself. We do not have any absolute means of verifying or falsifying the events described. We are left therefore with a number of possible options to try to account for what we might call Jesus' physical healing miracles.

First, we might wish to take an entirely agnostic line, arguing that too much time has passed since the events described for us to investigate them as thoroughly as we would wish. In addition, we might say that there is no external corroborating evidence contemporary with the events to help us come to a settled conclusion about what actually happened. In this case, we have to conclude that we do not have sufficient evidence to enable us to come to a reasoned judgement about what might or might not have occurred.

Second, we can ask whether the healing miracles, as described, seem to have an inner literary coherence with the rest of the narrative and suggest that, if they do, that might be a vote in favour of the miracles' plausibility. Even the most sceptical critic is likely to agree that the miracle stories pass the inner literary coherence test, but this does not mean that the events as described have a necessarily close relationship with what took place in reality. We have seen that in the construction of the gospels each author placed their own particular emphasis on the miraculous and did so to shape their own view of Jesus.

Third, there can be no doubt that Jesus' friends and family came to believe that his power and authority were derived directly from God. His healing miracles were seen by them as a sign of the breaking in of the kingdom of God. Following on from this, we might want to argue that in Jesus of Nazareth God himself was at work, and therefore, although God is beyond the limited powers of our own apprehension, we can and should expect the unexpected. Things which make no sense to us, from God's perspective might make perfect sense.

The difficulty with this argument is that it is marked by circularity. We are inclined to believe, say, that Jesus was God, and therefore interpret his activities in the light of that belief, and then go on to assert that the miracles are fine examples of Jesus' divinity, thus 'proving' that he was God.

Fourth, another argument is to say that the miracles were 'epiphanies', that is, manifestations of God's glory, where the eternal was breaking through into time, like the sun breaking from behind a cloud. Certainly, this is a powerful theme in John's gospel: the miracles are seen as moments of revelation when the God behind and within all things discloses himself in Jesus. But one of the questions, as we saw in the previous chapter, is what our criteria are for asserting that an event has the characteristics necessary for us to believe that it was a divine act. For example, the story of the healing of the Centurion's son (John 6:46–54), may be seen by one person as a miracle, while another sees it as coincidence.

It is clear that whichever of these views you hold, none of them is likely to persuade a sceptic that what we are dealing with here are real physical healings, real miracles.

How then can we proceed? It seems to me that we have to try to approach the miracle stories with as much integrity in our generation as the gospel writers did in theirs. We are not required to be gullible, nor are we required to believe a hundred impossible things before breakfast.

Suppose then we approach the miracles from our own perspective. We might begin by arguing that if there is a God, and if God is love, he is likely to be deeply involved in *all* healing of body, mind and soul. We do not expect 'normal' patterns of healing to fall outside God's care, as though it is only the inexplicable which counts; not at all. We do not rest our belief in God on divine acts, that is, extra-ordinary and inexplicable interventions by the divine in our ordinary lives; rather, we see God's activity revealed everywhere in all who care for the sick, in all research that is designed to lessen suffering, in all processes of healing.

We are also very aware, in our generation, that to divide healing into simple components such as 'physical' or 'mental' or 'spiritual' is to fly in the face of all the evidence that shows that healing is a complex and wonderful process involving body, mind and soul. And it is here that prayer needs to be mentioned. When we pray for a 'miracle' for someone who is very ill, what we are doing is associating ourselves with God's active love for that person. If God is God, and if God is love, then he will himself be profoundly engaged within that person at a deeper level than any of us can imagine. So by praying for the person we are not asking for special favours, we are trusting that God will be within and around the person and those who are doing the caring. More than that (and this is very difficult to put into words), many of us know that when we are prayed for, we are aware at a level beyond the rational that we are being upheld. Perhaps I can put it like this. Prayer has a kind of weight which does not burden but rather undergirds, and, as we are prayed for, that weight supports us. I know that it sounds paradoxical to talk about weight supporting us, but it is the best description I can give. It is, in my experience, how it is.

In addition, and this is a more philosophical point, we are heavily predisposed in our generation to find arbitrariness in God morally offensive. If a 'miracle' is granted to one person and not to another, that degree of arbitrariness offends our moral sensibilities. We have a high view of the necessity for God not to be arbitrary but to be just.

So where does this leave us in relation to Jesus' miraculous healings? We are probably still a bit uncomfortable with the so-called physical healings of Jesus, finding them intellectually puzzling, but recognise that we ought to keep an open mind about them. I suspect, however, that we might be entirely at ease with the notion that his healings were about the liberation of people from whatever shackled them, illnesses which had a profoundly psychosomatic character, and that this was achieved by the power of his authentic physical, mental and spiritual engagement with those who sought his help. In that sense, his healings were revelatory of the truth that God is deeply present with all who are sick and is incarnated in all works of healing everywhere. And it is precisely for this reason that we find the concept of 'miracle' as a special and exclusive act by God very difficult.

But all that I have written in the last few paragraphs needs to be seen in the light of what comes next.

For me, there are four awesome and huge events which truly deserve the name of miracle: first, creation – the fact that anything exists at all is astonishing; second, the incarnation of God in Christ; third, his death on the cross and his resurrection; fourth, his continuous love for us and his presence with us. All other so-called miracles, and our intellectual anxieties about them, fade into insignificance compared with those, and ultimately it is in the light of these four great miracles that we ought to think about the stories of Jesus' healings, and consider how he is present with us now.

6

Carers

ONE OF THE INTRIGUING things about the gospel stories of Jesus' healing miracles is how little we are told about those whom we might describe as the carers. Think, for example, of the man in the synagogue at Capernaum who was healed by Jesus (Mark 1:21–28). The story is told as a confrontation between the power of Christ and the havoc-wreaking effect of evil. But presumably the man involved had a family, or friends. There must have been someone who took him home afterwards. What did they say? Were they changed for ever by the experience?

Or, take the leper who was healed (Mark 1:40–45). There's no mention in that story of what happened to him afterwards. What did his friends make of him? Or was he so isolated by his disease that he had lost all contact with friends and family?

Just occasionally we get a glimpse behind the scenes; for example, in the healing of Peter's mother-in-law of a fever, we are told that as soon as she was better she waited on everyone (Mark 1:29–31). I have much sympathy for her. Wouldn't you feel hot and bothered if your son-in-law suddenly brought twelve hulking great men home for supper?

In Mark's gospel there are just five references to the carers in a healing story. There are the men who carried their friend on a stretcher to Jesus. As they could not get their friend through the door of the house because of the crowds, they had the bright idea of letting him down through the roof. It sounds like a kind of stag-night decision (see Mark 2:1–5). Then there was Jairus, the President of the synagogue, who sought Jesus' help because he and his wife believed that their little daughter was grievously ill (Mark 5:21–43). You can hear the anguish in his voice, 'My little daughter is at death's door, I beg you to come and lay hands on her so that her life might be saved.' It is the cry of every parent who sees their child in desperate need. There is, too, the Gentile mother originally from Phoenicia, who falls at Jesus' feet and begs his help. Jesus' reply is stern and hard, but the woman is feisty, determined that Jesus shall listen to her cry (Mark 7:24–30). And then, to complete the list, there are the friends who bring to Jesus a blind man in Bethsaida (Mark 8:22–26); and the father of the boy suffering from epilepsy, 'If it is at all possible for you,' says the man to Jesus, 'take pity on us and help us' (Mark 9:14–29). Again, you can hear how heart-felt the father's cry is. And that is it. No other carers get a mention.

But even in those few stories we can get a glimpse of the desperate longing many of them had. They really wanted the person they cared for to be well and took risks to get them what they believed to be the best help available. They were fighters. Perhaps, like many carers today, they felt a bit taken for granted and this helped them to take desperate measures. By the way, it would be fascinating to hear what the house owner had to say to the men who took his roof to pieces!

It is not possible to think of health and well-being without becoming aware that all who are sick are bound up with the lives of those who are well, and vice versa.

I once came across a greeting from (I think) South Africa which two people use when meeting. One says to the other, 'How are you? I am well if you are well.' It's a greeting filled with insight and human solidarity. And in the gospels we can see the same truth being expressed in a quiet but dramatic form in the account of Jesus washing the feet of the disciples. He bade his disciples to care for each other: 'If I, your Lord and Teacher, have washed your feet, you also ought to wash one another's feet. I have set you an example: you are to do as I have done for you.'

It is of the essence of Christianity that we are to follow the example of Jesus and care for those in need (think of the story of the good Samaritan); we are to be people whose lives are shaped and directed by love for God and love for our neighbour. And it is one of the insights of our faith that as we care for others so we are caring for Christ in them. It is a holy, demanding and privileged task, but it is also marked by one of the great and humbling mysteries of our faith – that as we serve others, so Christ himself serves us.

7

Meaning and purpose

In Diana Athill's autobiography, *Instead of a Letter*, she writes of the last days of her beloved grandmother. One afternoon her grandmother turned towards her and asked 'What have I lived for?'

Diana Athill writes:

It was she who should have been able to tell me that. All her life she had been a churchgoing Christian of apparently unshaken faith. But she was on her own then: not suffering like Doctor Johnson, from fear of the consequences of her sinfulness according to the teachings of that faith, but simply unsupported by it. I said to her what I believed: that she had lived, at the very least, for what her life had been. The long, hard months of dying could eclipse her life, but they did not expunge it. What she had created for us, her family, by loving and being loved, still existed, would continue to exist, and could not have existed without her. 'Do you think it has been worth something?' she asked, and I held her hands and told her that I believed it with all my heart. (Athill, 1963, p. 10)

The question of whether our lives have any purpose is one which can impact upon us at any time, and certainly comes at its fiercest when we, or someone we love, is suffering. There are a number of answers. Some will reply that life has no meaning apart from the meaning we ourselves give it. It is an honourable and brave answer. As one of my friends said to me on a cold winter's day when we had been discussing whether or not life had any purpose, 'I believe we have to put on our coats and just get on with it.'

For Christians, however, the answer is that there *is* purpose and there is meaning in life. Each time we say the Lord's Prayer, we say 'Thy will be done'. We believe that God is active in the world and part of our purpose is to share in God's work of healing and reconciliation. We see ourselves as part of a huge and overarching story – God's desire to reconcile the world and all its peoples to himself. It began at creation, was revealed in the stories and events outlined in the Old Testament, and became even more explicit in the life, death and resurrection of Jesus of Nazareth. We believe that this divine work continues through the ongoing and creative presence of the Holy Spirit. Our individual purpose, therefore, is to play our part in that astonishing narrative. In each generation we not only tell the story, we also try to become it.

Every Christian person, refreshed and renewed at their baptism, becomes, with their fellow Christians, an important and unique part of God's narrative. When we pray 'Thy will be done', we are saying that we want to go with the flow of that story, neither denying it nor stepping outside it.

For some people there is a strong sense that in order to do God's will they have to play a specific part in the story through becoming a priest or by joining a religious order. Others, with equal conviction and sincerity, have a strong sense that God has called them to express their discipleship in their daily work, in voluntary activities and in their relationships with other people. In my view, no vocation has greater importance than another; what matters is that we each try to live as God would have us live.

But there are times, as Diana Athill's grandmother found, when, in spite of regular attendance at church and a deep and conscientious faith, the sense of purpose disappears. Life suddenly seems utterly pointless and without any overriding purpose, and we feel no more significant than an insect whirling around the universe clinging on to the swaying planet which is our home. Following Christ does not protect us from human doubt or despair; in those circumstances what are we to do?

I do not believe that we should go into a state of denial and pretend that all is well, when it is not. Nor is it a matter of trying to convince ourselves by an act of will-power that we are not experiencing these feelings.

It could be that the feelings are a reminder of some unrepented, troubling sin and that this is God's way of gently calling us towards his grace and love; or, it might be a way of God leading us onwards into new territory, asking us to trust him even in the depths of our despair. You may remember that one of the most profound and searching books in the Bible is the book of Job, in which Job faces all kinds of suffering but waits with steely courage and patience for God to show him the way forward.

If intense feelings of despair are yours, it is worth repeating the truths of Psalm 139, in which the psalmist sees that no matter what is happening to him, no matter where he goes, God is always present:

> Lord, you have examined me and you know me.
> You know me at rest and in action;
> you discern my thoughts from afar.
> You trace my journeying and my resting-places,
> and are familiar with all the paths I take ...
> You keep close guard behind and before me
> and place your hand upon me ...
> Where can I escape from your spirit,
> where flee from your presence?
> If I climb up to heaven, you are there;
> if I make my bed in Sheol, you are there.
> If I travel to the limits of the east,
> or dwell at the bounds of the western sea,
> even there your hand will be guiding me,
> your right hand holding me fast.

St Paul in his great letter to the young church at Rome said something very similar:

> For I am convinced that there is nothing in death or life, in the realm of spirits or superhuman powers, in the world as it is or the world as it shall be, in the forces of the universe, in heights or depths – nothing in all creation that can separate us from the love of God in Christ Jesus our Lord. (Romans 8:38–39)

In times of despair, hang on to the truths in those verses and let them bring solace to your soul, for in our relationship with God, and God with us, is to be discovered our human meaning and our purpose.

8

Old age

THERE IS A STUNNING painting by Rembrandt of Simeon in the Temple holding the Christ-child in his outstretched arms. In the semi-darkness behind Simeon is the child's mother, Mary.

You will know the story in Luke's gospel. In the days after the birth of Christ, he was brought to the Temple in Jerusalem where a sacrifice was to be made according to Jewish tradition. In the Temple was a man called Simeon who is described by Luke as 'upright and devout, one who waited for the restoration of Israel, and the Holy Spirit was upon him. It had been revealed to him that he would not see death until he had seen the Lord's Messiah.' The moment Mary and Joseph appeared with the baby Jesus, Simeon took the child in his arms and burst out into a song of praise:

Now, Lord, you are releasing your servant in peace,
according to your promise.
For I have seen with my own eyes
the deliverance you have made ready in full view of
all nations:
a light that will bring revelation to the Gentiles
and glory to your people Israel. (Luke 2:29–32)

It was this moment of gracious epiphany that Rembrandt captured in his painting. The old man is radiant with wisdom and fulfilment; Mary is in the shadows, a reminder of the sorrow she will undergo when her son enters the shadow of death on Calvary; and the child is blissfully unaware of the life that lies ahead. In itself it is also a study of humanity: childhood, adulthood and old age. Rembrandt painted this picture when he was close to death, and it has something serene and full of hope about it.

He had painted another version of the Presentation when he was a young man. In that painting the scene is extraordinarily dramatic. The Temple is huge; a flight of steps, on which are crowds of people, provides the stage set for the encounter between Simeon and the Christ-child. A spotlight falls on the central scene. It is exotic, magnificent and grandiose.

When he painted the Presentation in his last months of life, Rembrandt had stripped the story down to its human essentials – an old man, a young woman and a baby.

In a sense, that contrast is a parable of how life changes as people age. At first, certainly in young adulthood, everything is potentially on a big scale. Life is great, buzzing and dramatic, filled with the excitements and challenges of the unknown. In old age, all of that experience is behind us. Life becomes richer, but not with a surfeit of *things*; rather, the richness lies in what is seen to be really important – families, friends, good health and happy relationships. More than that, because life inevitably begins to slow down, new interests emerge. There is time to cherish what is beautiful; time to think and reflect about the meaning of life; but also, let's not ignore the downside, there is time to grieve over mistakes made; time to ask whether the things one has done were of value; time to wonder about failures.

And then, there is also the fact that, statistically speaking, death is getting closer. There are things one might have done which are not now going to get done. Who knows how much time might be left? And, most disquieting of all, will the end when it comes be marked by suffering and humiliation, and not dignity? For those who are married there is also the question of who will be the one who is left, with all the desolation and grief and aching loneliness that that will bring.

Is there, in all this human muddle of joy and sorrow which characterises old age, a Christian set of attitudes or beliefs which will be a strength and comfort?

Let's not pretend that the journey will necessarily be easy. It has been the experience that some Christians have had that part of the human journey towards God involves a stripping down, a growth not in certainty but in uncertainty. It might be, for some of us, a time when we enter the darkness of unknowing, when we have to let go of assurance and rest simply and faithfully in the loving arms of Christ without having any real sense that he is truly there. Did not Christ himself on the cross cry out 'My God! My God! Why hast thou forsaken me?'

But we also know that God brought Christ through the searing anguish of death into eternity. It is this which surely marks us as Christian believers – that no matter what death might bring, death itself has been conquered by Christ. And it is in the light of this that we look with as much honesty as possible upon old age. It is as though the resurrection is like a light which casts its divine beams of glory backwards across our lives to illuminate what is already there, but also assures us that new life in eternity awaits us; not through any merits of our own, but solely by the outpouring and prodigal love which God has for us in and through Jesus Christ.

We should surely pray as Simeon prayed: 'Lord, now lettest thou thy servant depart in peace, for mine eyes have seen thy salvation …' To be able to pray that in old age, and at the end of our lives, will be a great blessing.

9

Death and dying

FIFTY YEARS AGO A book was written which had a great impact upon all who read it. It was called *A Grief Observed* and it consisted of the reflections that C. S. Lewis wrote after the death of his wife, Joy.

The opening sentences of that book are as follows:

No one ever told me that grief felt so like fear. I am not afraid, but the sensation is like being afraid. The same fluttering in the stomach, the same restlessness, the yawning. I keep on swallowing.

At other times it feels like being mildly drunk, or concussed. There is a sort of invisible blanket between the world and me. I find it hard to take in what anyone says, or perhaps hard to want to take it in, it is so uninteresting. Yet I want the others to be about me. I dread the moments when the house is empty. If only they would talk to one another and not to me.

C. S. Lewis wrote from a Christian perspective and throughout the book tries to make sense of where God might have been during this agonising period in his life. It is a book of real honesty. You can feel Lewis wrestling with his faith and his doubts unflinchingly.

In 2011 (fifty years after *A Grief Observed*), a delightful autobiography was written by Mirabel Osler. It too is a book of moral integrity, but is written from an agnostic perspective. In it Mirabel Osler writes of her family, their travels across the world, her children and grandchildren and the gardens she created. Towards the end of the book she writes of the death of her husband:

> I thought I had prepared myself for the day when, calling his name as I entered the house, I'd get no response. I used to look at Michael [*her husband*], asleep in an armchair, wearing his dressing gown, dying from a malignant brain tumour, and I'd think; this is the man with whom I have shared my life, our children, our love of poetry, good food and our garden. This is the man who has comforted me over countless sorrows, who has remained patient with my outlandish schemes. He is the companion with whom I've travelled, whose empathy I've depended on and from whom I am bracing myself to be forever deprived.
>
> However prepared you think you are, the finality of death cannot be rehearsed.

I have quoted C. S. Lewis and Mirabel Osler not to make a cheap and unjustifiable comparison between a

Christian believer and an agnostic (to do that would be to treat the integrity of both writers with exploitative disregard), but because in them both I found a courageous honesty about the finality of death, and searingly truthful descriptions of the grief of those left behind.

When we have loved, and our loved one has died, our grief, whether we are Christian or agnostic is equally terrible.

However, in the interests of honesty, and not for one moment wishing to treat with disrespect the views of those who are atheists or agnostic, there is a difference of underlying approach to death. Put simply, for a Christian, because of the life, death and resurrection of Christ, death is not regarded as the end. We believe in the resurrection of the dead, in life eternal, in coming to judgement before God, and, through his mercy and love, being swept up with the saints into the love and glory of heaven.

It is not that 'death is nothing at all'; quite the opposite. It is because we recognise the power that death has to bring us to absolute disintegration, to cause us not to exist, that we see with wonder the power of God, in Christ, to make all things new, to re-create us, to bring us out of the nothingness of non-existence into his glorious life.

In John's gospel, Jesus is quoted as saying this:

'Set your troubled hearts at rest. Trust in God always; trust also in me. There are many dwelling-places in my Father's house; if it were not so I should have told you; for I am going to prepare a place for you. And if I go and prepare a place for you, I shall come again and take you to myself, so that where I am you may be also.' (John 14:1–3)

It is in that hope that Christians place their trust.

This book has tried, albeit very briefly, to explore some of those big issues of health and well-being which we all face. It has approached them in the light of the beliefs of the Christian faith and has tried to show that Christian beliefs can withstand careful scrutiny, and can make a major contribution to our human self-understanding. It is also based on the premise that believers are required to be open in heart, mind and soul to new ideas and thinking and should explore health and well-being with humility and grace. While we have been given much by our forebears, there is still a great deal to learn.

Bibliography

Diana Athill, *Instead of a Letter*, Chatto and Windus, 1963 (Andre Deutsch, 1976).

Margaret Forster, *The Seduction of Mrs Pendlebury*, Secker and Warburg, 1974 (Vintage, 2004).

C. S. Lewis, *A Grief Observed*, Faber and Faber, 1961.

Mirabel Osler, *The Rain Tree*, Bloomsbury, 2011.

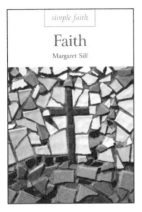

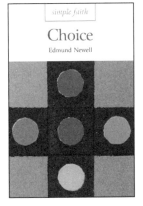